# THIS BOOK

## BELONGS TO

..................................................................

..................................................................

Thank you for Purchasing my book and taking the time to read it from front to back. I am always grateful when a reader chooses my work and I hope you enjoyed it!

With the vast selection available online, I am touched that you chose to be purchasing my work and take valuable time out of your life to read it. My hope is that you feel you made the right decision.

I very much would like to know what you thought of the book. Please take the time to write an honest and informative review on Amazon.com. Your experience and opinions will be of great benefit to me and those readers looking to make an informed choice.

*With much thanks.*

# Table of Contents

# Introduction

We all get stressed, regardless of who we are, where we come from, and what we do in terms of career and related personal endeavors. Lots of things have been divinely designed to put us in what some describe as a horrible condition associated with stress. This condition is due largely to our unending desire for things that may never even get to us.

Are we really the cause of our problem? Or is stress nothing but a normal process of life that is meant to help us grow stronger and better? What exactly is stress?

Is it just a mental/physical response to danger, pain, or opposition? Stress can cause many reactions in the body. What are these reactions, and how do they affect our lifespan? Have you heard about changes in heart rate, blood pressure, and gastrointestinal problems? Perhaps you have been told that a friend is suffering from one of the above conditions, or perhaps a physician told you some time ago to adjust your lifestyle because of one of these conditions?

These conditions are not what we're here to examine; rather, we're here to see how we can control their effect on our life. There are ways we can do this, if only we're willing to follow instructions and, where necessary, adjust to a life aimed at succeeding in stress rather than free from it.

Stress happens to your body when you have too much on your plate. It usually results from conflicts at work, family problems, or other kinds of emotional or physical happenings. It's a state of being in which you are constantly under pressure to keep up with what you're supposed to do, and it can be exhausting. Stress is a normal part of life, but it can take a toll on your mental and physical health if it becomes overwhelming.

In this book, we'll discuss how you can manage stress to live a more relaxed life.

# 1

# What Is Stress Management?

Stress management is a broad field that encompasses a range of techniques and psychotherapies. The goal of stress management is to control or reduce the chronic stress levels of a person. Although "stress management" is a broad umbrella term, it generally refers to the process of managing daily life and coping with stressful events. It is important to note that the goal of stress management is not to eliminate stressful events but to improve everyday functioning.

While some people attribute stress to subjective experience, physiological tests exist to measure the amount of stress a person is feeling. These tests are like polygraph tests and are commonly used to determine the level of stress. Using these tools can help a person design a stress management program that will address the root causes of their problems. Once these factors are identified, we can develop a program to target them and make appropriate interventions.

*Some of the most common types of stress are caused by natural disasters and major accidents in someone's life.*

Traumatic stress can cause distressing symptoms in a person, but these symptoms typically go away on their own. Things that would naturally result in traumatic stress include war, physical assault, major accidents, and related incidents. To effectively manage stress, there's a need to develop and learn coping mechanisms that will help you stop worrying about the future. This coping mechanism can help you avoid the chronic feelings of stress.

Fortunately, most people recover naturally from these situations. Stress management can also help you cultivate a culture of wellness at work and assist you in building a more resilient workforce. Studies have shown that companies with a healthy culture are more productive. This means that stress management programs can improve the overall productivity of an organization and make employees happier.

Stress management programs also make an employer look good.

While we are looking at stress management, it is important to **recognize** the **causes** of stress and learn to cope with them. Creating a stress journal can help you identify the things that cause you the most stress, and it is useful in managing your time and energy. It can also help you identify any triggers affecting your mental and physical health. While some types of stress are positive and can improve your life in many ways, some are a serious threat to your health.

**Acute** stress is a short-term reaction to a sudden event, while **chronic** stress can be a lifelong problem. It may cause you to develop heart disease or an abnormal heartbeat. You must learn to manage the effects of stress on your health and ensure that you stay healthy. Stress management techniques vary from person to person, and they can be useful in many situations.

The truth, however, is that stress management techniques should focus on dealing with particular situations. When different strategies are combined in managing stress, it can lead to a healthier and more productive life. A healthy life is more enjoyable and less stressful. The goal is to find a balance between work and relationships.

Fortunately, some methods of stress management are very simple. Some of these simple methods are more effective in dealing with personal issues, but they can also be generalized and applied in organizations. Ultimately, the most effective approach is to prevent stressful situations from happening in the first place.

A culture of well-being, they say, begins with managers. It may be impossible to escape stressful situations altogether, but being around other people can help. When stress management is done effectively, it can be a great way to improve employee performance and morale.

Stress management is a very useful tool for self-improvement in our everyday functioning. **Psychotherapies** and **relaxation** techniques help us tremendously in reducing our stress levels.

While there are many stress management methods, it is important that you know which is right for you. You will soon discover some useful methods that have been identified because of their effectiveness and popularity as stress management techniques. These techniques will help you manage stress and will improve your everyday functioning. So, get ready to enjoy your free time that is devoid of worrying!

*Stress management is a process that can help you manage your daily lifestyle and get better at handling stressful situations.*

You must learn to **focus** on the **present** and avoid worrying about the past. You must also learn to take things easy to have a more peaceful and stress-free life. By practicing effective stress management, you will be able to cope with the pressure of every situation in life. When your daily stress is effectively managed, you tend to live a life without worry or tension.

However, while focusing on managing stress is very beneficial, it should never be seen as a perfect solution in itself. Implementing the right strategies and techniques is sure to prevent the symptoms of stress and make it easier to deal with difficult situations, particularly those that seem to defy all reason.

There's a need to seek medical assistance when necessary, especially if you are experiencing extreme stress. It is vital to remember that sound health is the most important stress-preventing tool at your disposal in almost every stressful condition. Note also that the effects of prolonged stress on the human body are very unpleasant physically and emotionally. If you think you have a stressful work situation, it may be time to reduce your daily workload.

Stress can bring serious consequences to the quality of one's output. You must seek to prevent or manage its long-term health impact before it manifests in the form of physical symptoms.

Stress management can be very beneficial for a person's health. It is a good way to overcome stress and make life more manageable.

---

*Learn to avoid stressors, develop a positive relationship with people and make time for friends and family.*

---

The above is a proven method that will help you become more resilient to stress. Essentially, learn how you can stay away from stressful situations. It will help you minimize the adverse effects of stress and, as such, increase your productivity.

You must take care of your health, and try to reduce anxiety. One way to achieve this is to learn to talk to trusted friends and family when necessary.

Keeping healthy habits is essential for a healthy life. A proper diet is also very important. Any stress that does not affect your health is deemed to have been successfully managed. Generally, you should avoid smoking, drug abuse, and drinking excessively.

Moreover, you should be wary of consuming excessive caffeine because it affects your physical health and causes stress-related issues.

## Symptoms of Stress

Let's now look at some of the symptoms we may experience during stress.

Uncontrolled stress can cause four main types of symptoms. Our body responds to stress by releasing hormones directly into the bloodstream as part of our fight-or-flight response. This provides extra energy for our bodies. **Tachycardia**, which is an increase in heartbeats, is a result of increased adrenaline circulation.

## Physical Changes

If you've ever had a hard time sleeping, you know what stress is like. It can affect your physical and mental well-being, so it's crucial to know how to deal with it. A physical symptom of stress could be something like a stomach upset.

Anxiety can manifest in various ways and can make you feel irritable and unproductive. Often, we cannot sleep properly when stressed, and we feel rushed. There are many symptoms of stress. Physically, these may include headaches, dizziness, and a racing mind. Some people experience these symptoms only occasionally, while others may experience them more often.

Either way, it's important to seek help when you feel stressed. A healthy diet can help you cope better with stress. Try to incorporate at least thirty minutes of physical activity into your daily routine, even if it's just walking the dog. It's important to remember that chronic stress can lead to several medical conditions.

Although many people do not realize it, chronic stress can be detrimental to your health. If you have a high level of chronic stress, your body will produce hormones that make you feel sick. Your pulse will increase, and your muscles will be tense. You will likely have nausea, irritability, and stomach pains. Various symptoms of stress can lead to health problems. For example, people with chronic bowel disorders often experience high blood pressure and other related illnesses.

During traumatic events, a person's body may experience changes that affect their digestive health. This can harm their health over time. In addition to the physical symptoms, chronic stress can lead to depression, heart disease, and diabetes. Physical symptoms of stress are not always visible. Some people will experience muscle tension and difficulty making decisions. Sometimes, they may experience problems with their mental health.

While you may not have any physical symptoms of stress, it's important to recognize the signs and symptoms of stress. In addition, many people suffer from a mental health condition known as hypertension. It's also good to identify your peculiar symptoms of stress and to avoid stressful situations. For many, it could be insomnia, while others experience just headaches.

In addition to physical symptoms, stress can also happen internally. Self-induced symptoms of stress include excessive worrying and pessimistic thoughts. However, stress is arguably an important part of people's lives. As a result, it can negatively affect every system in the body. It is, however, essential to understand the causes and symptoms of stress.

You can prevent physical symptoms from surfacing by following a healthy diet. You can also take some steps to prevent the development of stress. A healthy diet is essential to manage stress and manage symptoms. It can also alleviate anxiety and depression. In addition, stress may also harm your mental health. It can affect your mood and interfere with your daily activities.

Note also that your symptoms of stress could be exacerbated by unhealthy eating habits. The physical and emotional symptoms of stress are often interrelated. Also noteworthy is the fact that your blood vessels dilate, causing your heart to become enlarged when you're in stressful conditions. With a healthy diet, your body can handle almost all types of stress and reduce its adverse effects. If you're down already, your overall state of health will improve dramatically once you start healthy eating.

Let me also add that while it's good for you to stay active, it is crucial to keep stress levels in check. The symptoms of stress are not limited to physical problems. For example, if you experience anxiety, you should seek help from an objective person. A trusted friend or colleague can help you understand your problems and help you reduce your stress. They can provide you with tips and advice on managing your daily stresses to reduce the risk of physical and emotional disorders.

What normally happens when your body responds to stressful events is the release of hormones known as adrenaline. Adrenaline changes autonomic nervous systems and gives the body an immediate burst of energy.

In certain situations, the fight-or-flight response can be triggered, which, in turn, triggers the release of cortisol and adrenaline. These hormones speed up your heart rate and shunt blood to major muscle groups. While these hormones are important for survival, they can be harmful over time.

Symptoms of chronic stress can be signs of other health problems, such as cardiovascular disease. Stress itself can be beneficial to our overall well-being, but excess of it causes damage that could seriously affect our health and relationships. If you feel you're not in control of your life, you're more likely to succumb to the effects of stress.

Although it can be difficult to identify the causes of stress, we must understand how it affects our life. Good stress comes from a single stressful event within a short period, while bad stress is a combination of many things occurring over a long period. When it's very prolonged, the body's normal physiological responses to stressful experiences become unproductive and harmful to the body.

This is why it's important to recognize the signs of chronic stress. **Acute** stress is the most common type of stress and can be caused by many situations, such as a car accident, and can be harmful if it is not treated. It affects all aspects of one's life, including how one looks and behaves. When acute stress is **chronic**, it harms your mental health and, in severe cases, leads to an **acute stress disorder**, which is an abnormal reaction.

Acute stress is a temporal problem and may not cause any permanent damage. In contrast, chronic stress is not, because it's a repeated acute stress condition. A good example of acute stress could be simple things like not meeting a deadline or a recent argument.

While the physical symptoms of chronic stress may not be strong, the severity can be exacerbated by emotional events. The most common workplace stressors, for example, are one's inability to complete work assignments, a demanding boss, and endless email threads. These factors all result in acute stress, a type of mental or emotional state that makes people feel overwhelmed or anxious that can lead to minor health problems, ranging from insomnia to a weak immune system.

**Chronic** stress is the opposite of acute stress. It is a prolonged situation, which can lead to serious physical problems. While the most acute stress is temporal, it becomes dangerous when it lasts longer than a week. At that stage, it can be fatal.

## Emotional Changes

Emotional changes that occur when we are in stress mode include increased irritability, a significantly higher sense of overload, inexplicable sadness, and a gradual sinking into depression.

## Behavioral Changes

The behavioral changes that we experience when stress levels exceed our control include changes in our social behavior, hygiene, and eating habits. Family, friends, and coworkers may easily notice these changes in behavioral patterns.

## Cognitive Changes

When our stress levels are out of control, we may be over-stressed. If that happens to someone else, we might notice cognitive changes in them. Uncontrolled stress can lead to lowered concentration, memory dysfunctions, and procrastination. This will also result in an inability to make decisions.

# 2

# Acute and Chronic Stress in Perspective

Acute stress and chronic stress are the two types of stress. **Acute stress** is an erratic, short-term condition characterized by high anxiety and a feeling of inevitability. Acute stress may be related to an underlying medical condition, but the main cause is specific. Below is some information about acute stress:

- Acute stress affects the body and can lead to physical problems.
- There are ways to effectively manage these conditions.
- Acute stress is characterized by negative thoughts about a recent event.
- Acute stress is experienced when confronted with a traumatic event or experience.
- Acute stress results in a breakdown or excessive competitiveness.
- Acute stress is temporary and will subside within a short time.
- Acute stress may be triggered by self-imposed demands, resulting in a high level of fatigue.
- Acute stress is common in people with type A personalities.
- Acute stress comes from an unexpected event or circumstance. Experiencing an extreme situation can change an individual's life and alter their beliefs.
- Acute stress can be excruciating, causing broken bones.
- Acute stress is the most common type of stress.

- Acute stress may cause headaches, abdominal pain, or dizziness.
- Acute stress can trigger physical or mental issues.
- Acute stress causes a person to worry a lot.

On the other hand, **chronic stress** can cause a person to feel physically ill. The body in chronic stress may have an inflammatory response that can cause health issues. This type of stress is more serious, hence the chronic kind. Acute and chronic stress are usually related to an event that happens too often. The main difference between these two is that acute stress is a short-term event, while chronic is long-term.

Stress can be classified as episodic and chronic when it's a repeated event or a result of uncontrollable behaviors. The worst cases of chronic stress can affect a person's daily functioning. Acute and chronic stresses are different in the way they affect the body. While acute stress may still cause ill health, the latter is characterized by long-lasting stress that is sure to cause ill health. It can be triggered by a single event or by repeated actions. Acute and chronic stress is relative to a person's environment and can cause an individual to feel irritable. It can be a symptom of depression or even a heart attack.

## Can Stress Be Useful?

It's natural to feel stressed out from time to time. While the term *stress* may seem negative, there are times that stress can be useful. In this instance, the body responds by producing more hormones that are useful for the body. When your body is exposed to high stress levels, it produces a more effective immune system. This is helpful, especially when you are faced with a stressful situation. This type of response can help you cope with any difficult situation better. When you feel stressed, your body's cortisol level rises.

This can lead to an improved sense of self and confidence. This is often beneficial when handling complex, stressful situations. For someone dealing with a complicated health condition, for instance, the ability to handle a stressful event can help them learn new skills and build mental toughness. This is why it's helpful to face stress. As they say, by facing your fears, you can gain a deeper appreciation of life.

When you feel stressed, your blood becomes sticky. This is a sign of the stress response, and if you experience chronic stress, your blood is less likely to clot. This is a good thing, but not if it causes a health problem. It's essential to avoid long-term or prolonged stress. It's important to note that stress can't help people who do not know how to handle stressful situations.

---

*Stress will help you to learn more quickly, because your body can process more information faster than normal during the process. In addition, stress hormones can improve your memory.*

---

When you experience extreme levels of stress, you may even lose weight. This is helpful for your health. And when you experience a manageable amount of stress, your body will be more alert and productive. This will make you more confident in your abilities and performance.

Some people believe that stress is not helpful. The truth is that long-term stress is bad for your health. If you're experiencing chronic stress, you'll want to get rid of it; otherwise, you'll be suffering from the physical and mental health effects of it. As you learn the good side of stress, it's important to understand that being under severe stress will reduce productivity in the workplace.

Stress can also be useful as it will motivate you to do things you've never done before. While this is useful in some situations, it may be harmful at other times. If you're prone to chronic stress, you should consider getting rid of it as soon as you can. This will allow you to work more efficiently in your routine and help you perform better in a new task.

Does it mean we won't have much energy to complete tasks if we are not stressed enough? That is not the point. The fact is that we need to find ways to reduce stress and improve our mood. If we don't deal with it well, it may become difficult to feel motivated.

If we can't handle the stress we face, it will affect our physical and mental health. It can even cause depression. Experts say that short-term stress is good because it keeps you motivated. The reverse is the case with chronic stress; you can't deal with the illness that comes with it.

Stress may help you stay focused if you suffer from mental illness, but severe stress can make you feel more confused. Stress without a symptom is usually not a source of concern for many; nevertheless, you should try to get your mind in a better state.

## Can Stress Be Harmful?

So far, we have noted that while short-term stress may be useful to one's socio-psychological development, it is generally harmful to one's health. At this juncture, it is important to understand the main difference between good and bad stress and what stress does to our body and brain. Unlike acute stress that doesn't take a huge toll on the body, chronic stress can affect the quality of our day-to-day living in terms of productivity.

We've already discussed the differences between the two types of stress and how each can affect our body system. The human body reacts negatively to extreme stress through heightened heart rate, increased blood pressure, and muscle tension. In addition to the physical effect, stress can also trigger emotional and mental responses. A medical doctor can provide a better explanation for these responses. Just note that although chronic stress can't be avoided entirely, it can be harnessed and monitored. Avoiding stress may not be practicable, but redefining how we react and adjust to it can be beneficial.

Some people experience stress more severely than others. The physical symptoms of long-term stress may include poor sleeping habits, memory loss, cardiovascular disease, and gastrointestinal conditions. Fortunately, there are also many ways to counter the effects of stress. There are a few simple steps you can take to reduce your stress. A healthy diet, plenty of sleep, and caffeine and alcohol reduction readily come to mind.

When necessary, one must consult a professional therapist to identify the possible sources of stress and cope with it. If you feel overwhelmed and unbalanced about certain conditions, consider forming a support system to buffer the damaging effects of stress and ensure you feel better. There is no cure for chronic, high-stress living, but there is always a way to manage it.

Chronic stress can be harmful to your health as it is long-lasting and can cause a person to feel miserable. Getting enough sleep and eating healthy foods are both essential ways to remedy the effect of stress. A person experiencing chronic stress can suffer from high blood pressure, ulcers, and headaches.

While positive stress keeps us alert and ready to fight the danger, negative stress can make us ill. The effect can be so severe in cases of post-traumatic trauma, which is a more serious condition. A constantly stressed person is prone to a host of physical and emotional problems. The best way to deal with these issues is to reduce the amount of exposure to stress as possible.

## The Concept of Stress and Burnout

"Burnout" was first introduced by Herbert Freudenberger in the 1970s. The American psychiatrist used burnout to describe the mental, physical, and emotional exhaustion experienced by members of the "helping professions" (psychiatrists, psychologists, counselors, social workers, and nurses).

New York psychiatrist Dr. Joynberger proposed that professionals who work in the helping professions may lose their motivation, and if not treated properly, they could succumb to depression. Freudenberger initially focused on helping professionals, but today, the term is used to refer to many similar cases in other sectors of private and public employment.

We see a lot of journalistic references to the "burnout syndrome" in both the printed and audio-visual mass media, beyond the traditional journals and areas where scientific research findings are often presented.

The battle that comes from stress and burnout is one of the most important comfort battles to wage in life. The constant pressure on the body is unhealthy for your emotional and physical well-being. Both are similar, but some characteristics differentiate them. Stress leads to anxiety disorders and depression. On the other hand, burnout is the result of too much work and demands, leaving a person feeling depleted and hopeless.

In many cases, people suffering from either of these two conditions may withdraw from their friends and family. While both conditions may have some form of advantage, stress is much easier to identify. For example, a close friend or colleague can't spot the signs of burnout. Even if they can see a difference in the person's energy levels, they can't pick up the subtle changes. While vacations may provide temporary relief, the right self-care strategies can help you build lasting resistance to stress and burnout.

Fortunately, both stress and burnout can be helpful. It can help you focus on performance and productivity. Working under high pressure can help you perform better. If you learn how to harness your innate skills under pressure, it can improve your work. However, when it gets to a certain level, you'll likely experience the signs of burnout.

Stress and burnout can be exacerbated by the same sources: inadequate communication, too much work, and a lack of support. As the present pandemic continues to rage, more people are working from home, and some are stressed because they're working longer hours. This increases the risks of burnout.

It is believed that if the source of stress is not addressed, burnout can lead to depression and even physical illness. It can also affect one's lifestyle. It could happen to anyone, not just to the professionals mentioned.

---

*The main difference between stress and burnout may lie in how you respond to it.*

---

While both conditions are common, they are not the same. The symptoms of stress can range from oversleeping to insomnia. The symptoms of burnout are often very similar to those of the latter. For instance, a person who experiences burnout may also have insomnia.

In some cases, people experiencing burnout may need to reduce the amount of time they work or find other ways to relieve their stress. They may have to change careers or cut back on their hours. For others, the problem could be something more serious, such as an overly demanding boss. To avoid this, it is best to seek help.

There are various treatments for both stress and burnout. In the case of burnout, an individual should consult with a psychiatrist and/or a professional therapist to get an accurate diagnosis. A person who experiences burnout may feel overwhelmed by the demands of their job. This can make it difficult to take action.

Although stress can be a legitimate part of life, the effects of burnout are often irreversible. In some cases, individuals may experience mental health problems, leading to job loss. Fortunately, both stress and burnout can be reduced and managed by taking positive steps. Regardless of the cause, it's important to seek help to manage the stress and stay productive.

If a person has too much stress, they can suffer from burnout. While it may not be physically damaging, it can have psychological consequences. A person who is experiencing burnout may have difficulty concentrating and focusing. They may forget things easily and experience a lot of psychosomatic complaints.

Professionals suffering from burnout may find themselves unable to complete their job. In addition to a reduced ability to work, people who experience chronic stress have symptoms similar to those associated with the onset of dementia. While most people are aware of their stress, they are unaware of their burnout.

In contrast, individuals suffering from burnout are often unable to identify the difference between the two conditions. The symptoms of stress and burnout are usually not very noticeable, but they are often related to a lack of motivation and unhappiness. Moreover, a person suffering from burnout might find it difficult to work or live.

When an individual is in this situation, it becomes hard to connect with others.

## What Are the Causes of Stress?

In our distant ancestors' daily lives in the primitive grasslands or primeval forests, there were likely stressors like the need for food, shelter from the elements, and the ability to deal with many other difficulties. We, you, and I can all testify that modern multicultural societies where we were born and raised have a multitude of stressors that can catch us off guard. These stressors include losing a bus or train in a rush, being stuck on a busy road, missing an interview, or being late for a date.

It's not an exaggeration to say that stressors are in the thousands for some people and hundreds for others. It could be something happening in a very short period or over a long period. Many aspects of our daily lives can lead to external or internal stress.

External stressors for young people are often related to school, grades, performance requirements, interpersonal relationships, and romantic relationships. Stress can also be caused by a person's parents or siblings. Young adults and mature people are more likely to experience stress from external sources, such as financial worries or difficulties with their supervisors and peers at work.

Stressors in the family can arise from friction with the spouse or partner, as well as child problems if the parents are involved. Stressors can be caused by internal issues that affect our **personality** or **psychological makeup**. This can lead to stress for all of us and require proper treatment and solutions. Some people find themselves under stress due to their **unrealistic goals** and difficulty achieving them. Some people tend to be perfectionists, while some may be perpetual worriers who cannot accept the reality of their circumstances, adjust, and be happy.

There are indeed some stressors that can be very difficult for us all. There are many negative stressors, such as dealing with the death or serious illness of a loved one or being laid off from work. We also encounter positive stressors like planning for an engagement party and going to our first day at work.

Minor stressors can be managed by most people, but they may pose a serious problem for others. In other words, it is not just the severity of the stressor that matters but also our psychological makeup, personality, and behavioral patterns in dealing with the different stressors.

Stressed people are less able to manage their responsibilities. This can lead to more stress and worsening of the situation. Stress is a common experience for everyone. It can cause headaches, high blood sugar, and more.

In addition, a person who is under a lot of stress may also be prone to substance abuse. Acute stress is also a natural part of life, and it is often helpful in dealing with the effects of new experiences.

There are many causes of stress. One of the most common is a **fight** between two friends. An **argument** could end in tears or cause a breakup. An unrelated situation, such as a traffic jam, may not be the root cause of your stress. Another common cause is a physical injury, like a car accident. These factors are often self-generated. It's important to remember that a person's reaction to a stressful situation can greatly differ. During a traumatic event, the brain's activity increases.

It also signals the body to prepare for danger. This type of stress results in several physical and mental health problems. This condition is called chronic stress; however, it is not limited to these two reasons. For example, the causes of chronic stress are varied, and it can result in serious physical symptoms and depression. Nevertheless, it is important to know what makes a person feel stressed.

In a nutshell, the chronic stress a person experiences may be due to the following three factors:

- The first factor is those that influence the body's ability to cope with stress.
- The second factor is the ability to control the physical response to the situation.
- The third factor is a person's environment.

In such cases, the external causes of stress will determine whether a person is more vulnerable to the effects of chronic stress.

The most common causes of stress include **relationships** with **family members** and work. The stress experienced by an individual can be a result of a demanding boss, a difficult job, or a traumatic event. Some people may also feel extra stressed because they are in the middle of a family emergency. They may also feel that they cannot keep up with their family life. It can be difficult to maintain a good work-life balance as there are many causes of stress.

While there are many other causes of stress, there are some common reasons for the presence of chronic stress. Some of these sources are **guilt,** the **desire** not to disappoint people, and a lack of time. Also, having too much time can make a person feel tired too. It is impossible to deal with stress if the cause is not identified and treated. Chronic stress can also lead to a coma.

When a person experiences a **traumatic event**, they will likely experience stress. Most people experience two kinds of stress: an acute type, which is triggered by a situation that creates an immediate response of panic, and the chronic type, which is a result of a severe case of a stressful situation.

**An unhappy marriage** or a difficult job is a source of stress. Other people may feel chronic stress due to circumstances beyond their control. In this case, the cause of chronic stress is difficult to explain. An acute form is usually caused by a single large pressure or event. While the latter is caused by a gradual buildup of small pressures and emotions, long-term uncontrolled stress is caused by a series of minor, recurring problems.

The body responds to the stressor by increasing its blood pressure, releasing a flood of hormones. Chronic stress is difficult, but it can still be managed.

## Are Some People More Vulnerable?

To effectively determine this, more research is needed. Some people are genetically predisposed to stress, and there are some facts to support this assertion. Research shows that mothers who have been through serious stress during pregnancy are more likely to transfer excessive stress hormones to the fetus, making it more difficult for the child to have a good tolerance to stress.

Many factors can be associated with stress. These are your **family health history**, **stressful life events**, **thinking style and poor coping skills**, **personality**, and **lack of support** from the social network. Even if geneticists discover more biological possibilities, stress can be caused by many factors.

It is important to realize that a predisposition doesn't necessarily mean you are destined for it, so don't consider it a death sentence. An example is that an individual could be predisposed to heart disease. The person may not develop it sooner if they engage in a healthy lifestyle and exercise regularly.

# 3

# General Tips for Stress Management

Managing stress can be a difficult task. While many techniques can help you deal with your situation, the first step is to talk to your healthcare provider. Learn your limits and ask for help if you need it. If you are having difficulty managing your stress, consider joining a support group or getting counseling services. You can also ask for advice from a friend or family member. These strategies will make stress management easier.

To effectively manage your stress, you're advised to **start small**. It may sound counterintuitive to talk to a doctor, but taking action at the moment will be the best way to lower your blood pressure and reduce your heart rate.

Taking action is essential to avoid feeling overwhelmed as the symptoms build up. When planning for upcoming events, start small and work your way up from there. The goal is to avoid the feelings of being overwhelmed.

Another tip for stress management is to limit your workload. This will reduce your feelings of being overwhelmed. By refusing to take on additional projects, you will be able to handle your stress levels.

**Being assertive** will also help you cope with your anxiety. When you feel overwhelmed, you should say no. You can also limit the time you spend alone. By saying no to extra requests, you can avoid getting too overwhelmed.

Using a **stress diary** can help you identify stressful situations. This will help you avoid procrastinating. Using a stress diary is an excellent way to track what's going on in your life. Keeping a diary can also help you stay organized and on top of your assignments. It is important to have a schedule, even if you're under a lot of pressure.

It is also important to **keep yourself motivated**. There are many other techniques that you can use to manage your stress. The first step, however, is to take stock of your situation. During stressful times, it's important to think about the long-term impact on your health. You need to look at your situation positively and keep things in perspective.

**Exercise**. By doing so, you'll be able to find ways to relax and reduce your tension. Physical activity releases chemicals that relieve anxiety and reduce body pain.

Other strategies for stress management include **guided imagery** and **listening to music**. Aside from this, guided imagery can be very helpful in reducing stress. When you're stressed, your mind can't focus on anything, so you need something to help you stay calm and focused.

Similarly, **identifying** and **managing your problems** is the key to success. By coping with your problems, you can achieve the highest level of productivity. If you're suffering from depression, you should find a way to relieve your stress and improve your health.

There are many ways to deal with your stress. By **learning** to **identify the source** of your stress, you can implement strategies to help manage it. If you're worried about the evening news, you should stop watching it. If you're a chronic shopper, shopping online and avoiding traffic will also help.

In addition to these, you should **limit your contact** with people who cause you stress. By doing so, you'll prevent certain problems from becoming bigger problems. If you're dealing with a stressful situation, you should consider using **relaxation techniques** to deal with the stress. Using relaxation techniques can help you to sleep better.

It is also helpful to **practice meditation**. Things like yoga and meditation can also be used to manage your stress. Indeed, lots of proven techniques to manage your stress exist. While these techniques may be simple, they are very effective. If you're not familiar with them, read books that carefully explain them. You will learn some important tips for stress management.

Stress management is an essential part of life that can help you with your stress levels and provide many other benefits to enhance your well-being. You can be more productive if you're able to relax. Developing a balanced life is important in maintaining your health.

By extension, this can help you live a happier and more stress-free life.

## How to Identify Stress Sources

To identify your stress source, start by making a list of all the situations in your life that are likely to trigger you to become stressed. While many people have a problem identifying the exact source of their stress, others can easily recognize it because they regularly experience chronic or episodic stress.

*To manage your stress, you must recognize a common pattern in your life.*

Apart from your work, you should also keep track of your social life and other things that make you feel stressed. If you are unsure how to find your stress source, you may seek a therapist's advice.

Having a therapist or counselor can help you determine the exact source of your stress. The experts will also help you create a healthy schedule to manage whatever you're facing. When you do this, you'll be able to deal with stress regularly. Even if you don't need professional assistance, it is recommended to identify your source of stress to make healthy changes.

Once you've identified your source of stress, you can take steps to deal with it. You might need to let go of some of your responsibilities or ask for help. Some people may find it helpful to take on a hobby they enjoy.

If you have **low self-esteem**, you may be prone to chronic stress. While you may feel that you can cope with this type of stress on your own, you'll find that you can't avoid stressful situations easily. Identifying your stress source is the first step in solving your problem and living a happier life. No matter the kind of stress, the same techniques can help you manage it so you can live a more balanced life.

Categorically stated, chronic stress is not healthy for your heart. You should find a way to deal with it effectively to reduce stress levels.

If your stress is acute, you should avoid a stressful environment. Once you've identified the source, you can address it more appropriately.

## Stress Source Identified—What's Next?

When you identify your stress, you should see a doctor or therapist. They can prescribe medicine that will help you manage it. They will also help you identify more sources of stress in your life and reduce the symptoms of long-term stress through guidance and counseling if you're dealing with chronic stress.

A family member or close friend is a good place to start when you're struggling with stress. Once you identify the source of your stress, you can develop strategies to overcome it. Sometimes it can be internal and difficult to recognize. Some people are more sensitive to external causes of stress than others. You might be surprised by the fact that a person can be stressed by small things but not by bigger things.

Other causes of stress can be self-induced and hard to explain to others. Regardless of the cause, it's important to identify your stress source and manage it accordingly. If your source is an uncontrollable factor, then you'll need to take steps to reduce it. It's important to determine which type of stress is causing your feelings of tension. If you feel that your stress is coming from a relationship, you may be feeling the strain in your marriage. Once you have identified your stress source, the next step is to eliminate it. This is a necessary step to reduce the risk of burnout.

If your stress problem is not alleviated, it can lead to burnout or an ailment. While an acute stress source is caused by a single traumatic event, it's best to find the source of the problem and remove it. If the stress is caused by an ongoing stress condition, then you can work with a therapist to manage it.

The simplest method to deal with stress is to identify the causes and reduce its effects. When you're experiencing stress, you'll find many signs. You might feel irritable, or you might even experience stomach upset. You need to learn how to handle your stress. If you're dealing with your boss, try to make sure you're not putting yourself under too much pressure. This way, you'll be more likely to keep your cool and avoid the problems that cause your stress.

# 4

# How to Recognize a Stress Signal

Learning to recognize a stress signal is vital in dealing with chronic or acute stress. There are various physiological changes associated with stress, as have already been mentioned in previous pages: the increased heart rate, difficulty in breathing, headaches, and the likes. To avoid experiencing these changes, it is important to know what triggers your stress. It is also beneficial to recognize and manage the causes of the stressful state. The ultimate goal here is to manage your stress to improve your overall health. The key is to always avoid situations that can make you feel stressed.

In trying to recognize a stress signal, a person can easily mistake a symptom of stress for another ailment. It is important to identify your symptoms and seek medical attention if they persist. Remember, your body's ability to detect a stress signal depends on genetics. If you're not aware of the symptoms associated with your particular type of stress, it will be difficult to reduce them.

Recognizing the signs of stress is an important step in managing stress. Depending on the nature of your condition, your reactions to different situations may vary. Observe how your body responds to each type. If you have high expectations, you may be under a lot of stress. If you're unable to meet them, your brain may not function properly. Being under a lot of stress could lead to many negative effects, such as a breakdown or an injury.

Knowing the stress signal is crucial to identifying the cause of stress and combating it. While recognizing a stress signal may not be easy, knowing the signs of chronic stress can help you deal with it more effectively. Your symptoms may be different from those of acute stress. You may experience increased social withdrawal or related issues that will make you recoil to yourself without knowing exactly what is happening to you.

Moreover, it is important to learn how to recognize the symptoms of stress. Some physical symptoms are often a stress signal. You may experience overthinking, worrying, or other behavioral changes associated with a highly stressful environment. In such situations, you might experience anxiety.

To say the obvious, the breakthrough in managing a stress response is to recognize the symptoms. This means knowing how to identify the symptoms. After which, it is also essential to quickly treat the underlying causes to avoid the possible conditions that often arise. Sometimes you may feel physically stressed with a high heart rate. This may be because you are suffering from a disease.

A person suffering from a severe stress response may not experience a severe stress reaction. If you have low self-esteem, for instance, you may have trouble recognizing a stress signal. You may feel that you have little control over your life, although every stress signal is not necessarily an immediate warning. You need to understand the symptoms before anything chronic takes center stage.

You already know that you can become depressed or sick if you are strained. You should avoid situations that cause you to feel overwhelmed and irritable. If you are constantly in a stressful situation, the stress can cause you to have difficulty sleeping or working.

Once you experience a hint of stress, you must treat the problem with a positive attitude and immediately take action. It will also be helpful to talk to a doctor if you are not sure what is causing the symptoms. A physician will determine whether you are suffering from a condition related to depression or chronic anxiety. So if you are feeling overwhelmed in a way, the best thing is to find a therapist or counselor.

## Recognize and Develop a Stress Strategy

It's always good to have a strategy of overcoming every issue in life, including stress-related matters. Once you have recognized and developed a strategy, it will be easier to handle. While it may seem strange to write down a list of things to do when you feel stressed, you can still do it, as it will help you better understand your behavior. It is good to note that if you can recognize the underlying cause of your stress, you can deal with it much more effectively. In other words, you should not ignore the signs that you are experiencing.

Managing your stress can be a tricky task. Despite the many ways to cope with it, your best option is to acknowledge that you are facing a stressful situation and that you need a strategy to overcome it, whether as a parent or a spouse.

## Implementing Healthy Stress Management Strategies

Knowing how to effectively carry out healthy stress management may be difficult for many. Most people would find it difficult to understand the concept, so they don't talk about managing it. Some **daily behaviors** can temporarily reduce stress.

Many people who try to cope with stress unknowingly engage in unhealthy behaviors, making the problem worse. Every individual reacts to stress differently, and you must find yours and determine how best to approach it.

If you have understood your peculiar symptoms, you will soon learn that your body processes stress in different forms.

Let's assume that you now understand how your body responds to different types of stress and want to start practicing stress management to reduce the effect. You may have read some books and noted that while some management techniques might be effective, they may not work for you.

To be sure you're using the right strategy, you can try to understand a concept I would describe as your **body's stress tolerance** level. People with a low tolerance for physical discomfort may not want to do strong body exercises, but the good news is that there's always something you can try. The famous **breathing exercises** come in handy here.

Everyone is different in terms of the capacity to handle things that have to do with emotions. "Don't take on more than you can handle." This advice is applied in almost everything we do in life, including stress management, so we must learn to **ignore certain things**.

Always analyze and prioritize tasks according to importance. Remember that you must have a working schedule if you're trying to reduce the work you do. And if you're overwhelmed while on any job, you must try to adjust either by cutting down on your to-do list or eliminating the entire process, if it is all you need to have a healthy work-life balance.

Things around us (environmental factors) sometimes are a major source of stress. **Habit** is a huge factor as you plan your overcoming strategy. Certain things we do to feel happy and satisfied may not be the best if we're looking for a way out of this quagmire.

Things like:

- overeating,

- excessive drinking,
- excessive caffeine intake, and
- long hours watching TV

These activities, though arguably may help relieve stress in some people, can also be a source of concern for many.

It's important to practice what is best for you. You may have to experiment with a few methods before finding the right one that suits your lifestyle and needs.

As you already know, there is no way to completely avoid stressful situations; you can just try to avoid them by focusing on those that you can control.

Prominent among them should be:

- Work: how and where you work
- Relationships: who you relate to and who you relate with
- Habit: what you do and how you do it
- Health: knowing when to stay calm and when to see a doctor
- Diet: what to consume and the right quantity to consume that will not be adverse to the body

*Learn to do things that will keep your health and, by extension, your life, intact.*

Apart from addressing your individual needs, you should consider, as a priority, your work environment and the people who work there. Your work environment should be a place that promotes a healthy work-life balance. A healthy work-life balance, they say, begets a relationship that will make you calm and productive.

Any healthy strategy you are using should be able to handle whatever you face. Most importantly, it should prepare for situations and minimize their adverse effects.

---

*Remember, your ultimate goal is to be able to cope with, and not to eliminate, stress.*

---

Most people say they don't know that stress is a silent killer. You can protect your health by having a proper schedule and implementing a healthy stress management plan.

# 5

# Workplace Stress

Multiple studies have shown that adults are stressed primarily by their jobs or the need for money. This kind of stress is recurrent and has been on a steady rise over the past decade. Increased demands have been linked to higher rates of hypertension and heart attacks.

Workplace demand constitutes a major source of concern for many people, especially young adults, with a possibility of harmful physical and emotional responses. This is even worse if there is a conflict between job demand and the worker's individual needs.

In general, a highly demanding job is stressful on its own, and workers frequently have no control over the situation. Workplace stress can come from many sources. Unfortunately, the impact is on the employees and employers because of the relationship between input and output (productivity).

Some people refer to workplace stress as a "challenge" or what is referred to as "positive stress." However, if this kind of stress occurs in a way that you cannot handle, mental or physical changes may occur, which is something you don't want to experience.

## Managing Workplace Stress

Those who can manage work-related stress say that it helps them to stay alert, focused, and motivated for new challenges at any time. It seems the case, though, as it keeps you alert and on the right side of your audience.

In today's fast-paced world, too many people feel anxious, depleted, or overwhelmed by the demands of their job, which range from working long hours to having tight deadlines. Almost everyone is looking for a better way to harness these inherent challenges to their advantage.

Managing workplace stress is an act that you have to master. Although you may not control every aspect of your workplace, it doesn't mean you are powerless. It simply means that it's time for you to take action. Stress at work has a way of affecting your **personality** and **career growth**.

There are many things you can do, regardless of what you do as job specifications at the workplace. Your goal is to do things that will lower your stress levels to be in control of your work environment.

**Share your feelings with people who care.** Sharing your stress with your significant other, friends, and family can be a great stress reliever. This is because you can get useful support, especially if done with face-to-face communication. It has been said that talking about your issue with those who care may not fix your problems; it's the knowledge that the other person knows about your situation that matters. In most cases, you will discover, surprisingly, that the person also has something unique to say about their condition.

Talk to **coworkers** for support. A solid support system can buffer you from the negative effects of job stress on your health. Remember to listen to your coworkers and offer support when they need it too. You can make an effort to socialize with colleagues. Just know that talking about it can help you manage it.

Instead of looking at your phone during the break period, you can unwind through useful engagement with colleagues.

Be closer to your **family** and **friends** as this has been proven over time to be a great way of managing not just workplace stress but all aspects of life. The flip side is that the more lonely and isolated you are, the more vulnerable to stress you will be.

Make **new, satisfying friendships**. You can meet new people by joining a class, taking part in a club, volunteering your time to support a cause, and expanding your social network. You can also help others, especially those who are appreciative. It delivers immense pleasure and can help you to significantly manage stress.

## Shift-Related Workplace Stress

You may experience sleep disturbances from working night shifts, early morning shifts, or related shifts. This can affect your productivity and performance, making you more susceptible to stress. This is so because the bright light at night can't help you adjust your sleep-wake cycle.

The sunshine naturally doesn't promote sleepiness, but you can wear dark glasses when you return home, to prevent sleep deprivation. **Limit** also the **number** of **irregular** or **night shifts** you do in a row. You should avoid rotating shifts too often so that you can keep the same sleeping schedule. **Reduce light** and **noise** in your **bedroom** during the **day** by using blackout curtains, a sleep mask, earplugs, or a soothing sound device to block out the daytime noise.

Very useful task management tips for reducing job stress will include the following:

- Prioritize your tasks.
- Focus on high-priority tasks before doing others.
- Do not wait until you are miserable before stopping what you are doing.
- Break down large projects into milestones. Don't try to do everything (even if you can) at once.

- Share responsibility, as it's okay to delegate.
- Don't try to control everything, even if it's in your control.
- Learn to be open to compromise so you can flow along with people.
- You and your boss can work together in adjusting expectations.
- Get rid of bad habits that lead to stress at work.

Try doing this at all times, as it will allow you to let go of unnecessary stress.

Negative thoughts and behaviors can make job stress worse. **Employer-imposed** stress will be easier to manage if you change your **self-destructive habits**.

---

*Don't be a perfectionist. You will fail if you set unrealistic goals.*

---

Do your best because no one will do that for you. Turn your negative thinking around. Stop focusing on the negatives in every interaction or situation. It will drain you of energy and motivation.

**Positive thinking** is key. Avoid **negative coworkers** and congratulate yourself for small achievements.

You can't control everything at work, especially if it has to do with the behavior of others. It pays to mind your business by focusing on what you can control.

Find **humor** in situations. Humor is a great way for people to relax in the workplace. Share a joke or funny story with those around you, as long as it does not affect your job.

**Get organized** as it makes things easier, saves time, and reduces stress. Champion initiatives in your workplace that you think are worthwhile. The obvious fact is that our stress levels rise when we feel helpless, uncertain, or out of control.

As an option, **discuss workplace stressors** with your **employer**. Happy employees are more productive. Your employer knows this, so they should have an incentive to reduce workplace stress. Instead of complaining about everything, tell your employer the exact thing that is affecting your work's performance.

If it has to do with job specification, make sure you clarify it with your superior. You can get a copy of the guidelines from your supervisor or any other person in that capacity.

Discuss your job responsibilities broadly, as it is possible that some of the tasks you have been doing are not part of your job description. You can leverage dialogue to point out that you have been working beyond the scope of your job.

**Requesting** a **transfer** is an option, but you might be able to escape from toxic surroundings by moving to another department. You can also request for an entirely **different responsibility** if you think the former is causing you more trouble.

**Take some time off work** if you feel that burnout is inevitable. Go on vacation, use up your sick days, or ask for a temporary leave of absence…just do anything to remove yourself from the situation. The above, mentioned in the workplace, is designed to help workers relax and get a breath of fresh air from routine.

Find **meaning** and **satisfaction** in your work, as experiencing dissatisfaction with your work can lead to stress. Many of us dream of a job we love and find rewarding even when we aren't in a position to search for a new career. It's normal, and, with more effort and proper planning, most of us can still find meaning and joy in a job we don't like.

Even the most mundane of jobs can be a great place to focus. Even if you only have to chat with your coworkers at lunch, focus on the aspects of your job that you enjoy. You can also change your attitude toward your job to regain control and purpose.

## How Employers and Managers Can Reduce Stress at Work

An employee who is suffering from work-related stress may have a lower productivity rate. As an employer, you can reduce workplace stress by first being a **positive role model**. It's easier for employees to emulate your calmness in stressful situations. Consult with your employees. Talk to them about what makes their job stressful. Some issues, such as **equipment failure**, **understaffing**, or **lack of feedback from supervisors**, may be easy to fix. Information can be shared with employees to reduce uncertainty regarding their future careers. Talk to your employees one-on-one if you can. It will help them feel heard and understood, even if it's impossible to fix the situation. This will reduce stress for both you and the workers.

To positively manage workplace **conflicts,** set a zero-**tolerance policy** for harassment. Provide workers with opportunities to take part in decisions that impact their job. Ask employees for input about work rules. They will be more engaged if they are involved in the process.

Don't set unrealistic deadlines; be realistic about your staff's abilities and resources. Properly define your expectations. Identify the roles and responsibilities of employees, and make sure that management actions are consistent with organizational values and are fair.

Provide **incentives** and **rewards**. A reward system that applauds work achievements verbally and organizationally is good. You should schedule periods that can be stressful and then have periods with shorter deadlines. Provide opportunities for social interaction among employees too.

## Causes of Workplace Stress

Many things cause workplace stress:

- Conflict within the workplace
- A poor physical environment
- A lack of communication
- Overwork
- Lack of physical exercise

Although in no particular order, these all contribute to workplace stress. Fortunately, there are ways you can reduce them in the workplace. Indeed, they are a free method with no side effects, and they're also easy to implement.

**Overwork** is a result of a shortage of staff or a lack of appropriate resources. As much as employers must ensure that employees are engaged in their work, they should also make sure that the work, though challenging, is not overwhelming. Provide some **autonomy** and learning opportunities.

Lack of **communication,** as a cause of workplace stress, can be corrected through proper and improved communication. Poor communication can lead to wrong results and a stressful working environment.

If an employee's **income** is low, it can cause stress. It's even worse if the company is unclear about its financial obligations. Employees may not want to seek legal help because they are simply afraid of losing their jobs. The truth again is that most people are looking for the best-paying jobs. The best way to eliminate this kind of low-wage work stress is to have employment agencies properly document your contract with a company with the best salary structure.

If that's not possible, try looking on the internet for the most profitable jobs. Many people are stressed out about their jobs. Whether they have to deal with too much work or are too overwhelmed, workplace stress is a serious problem. It affects the health and productivity of employees, so it's essential to take measures to reduce the burden.

There are many ways to manage workplace stress. As a business owner, you can take proactive measures to reduce the pressure and help staff stay productive.

If work is done in a highly stressful environment, workers may experience constant conflicts with coworkers. The lack of collaboration with colleagues can make one feel stressed and depressed. Not everyone can cope with this kind of issue.

When you're under constant stress, it's difficult to make decisions. If you're experiencing workplace stress, you may not be able to concentrate, or you may become easily distracted while doing your job. Your physical state and, finally, your health are also affected.

Having less time to relax can be detrimental to your health, especially if your job involves working in a stressful environment. Even if you're not a victim of this issue yet, you should consider the potential risks and a possible adjustment strategy.

Remember to always ask for help from a relevant authority when necessary. You might be surprised to find that the person you're afraid of is willing to assist you. From things like more time to finish a project to requesting more training, some employers are more willing to help.

The **management style** and the nature of the work environment are common causes, too. Rapid changes in policies and a lack of advancement opportunities can be stressful to workers. It often makes them feel displaced and unsupported.

An employer's policy and practices should be family-friendly. If these are not in place, employees often suffer psychologically and leave the company in the middle of a project.

## Dealing With Workplace Stress

Workplace stress is not difficult to detect if you pay attention to it. As stated already, you may have difficulty concentrating and starting a project due to a lack of motivation. It's not uncommon for some people to try to use drug-related substances to overcome work-related stress.

Many people go through this kind of problem as part of their daily routine. By merely looking at some people, you will know they are battling stress because the physical symptoms are noticeable. In others, the symptoms are psychological, so it is hard to know what they are going through. It can be severe and negatively affect productivity if the stress is not well managed.

As in almost all stress-related cases, it is important to get **enough rest** and avoid overworking yourself. It's also important to eat a balanced diet before and after each working period. You may not realize just how fast workplace stress can affect your health. Once your blood pressure rises, your cholesterol increases, and your immune system is weakened.

Once the immune system is down, other minor health issues will start developing as physical signs. You might notice very simple and usual things like strange rashes on the skin.

Is this a source of concern? Yes and no depending on who is involved, as a person's capacity to handle stress differs. The sooner you address these issues, the quicker you can get back to your optimum production capacity.

As noted also, familiar symptoms of stress might be some other medical conditions, hence the need for early intervention.

**Occupational therapy** may be an effective way to address workplace stress. It is best to speak to your HR department to learn about your legal obligations. You should consider seeking help from an occupational therapist if you're experiencing symptoms of workplace strain. While some changes can be made on your own, others will require the cooperation of others.

Now, as a worker, what exactly is causing you stress? Can you think of anything? Perhaps

- you're forced to work longer hours,
- you feel overworked because of pressing demand, or
- you're underpaid, considering your high input.

You can always manage this kind of challenge since the sources are known. All you need is the knowledge of what to do. You can just start with eating a healthy diet, doing regular physical exercise, and getting enough sleep as part of your effort toward managing stress.

# 6

# Employer's Role in Preventing Workplace Stress

Preventing workplace stress as an employer is essential to the health of your employees and the community in general. Experts suggest a proper destigmatization of the subject. People under work-related stress may not show signs of distress, like low morale, but they may have a problem handling deadlines or negotiating with bosses. They should be allowed to seek professional counseling or a career change to prevent further deterioration of their health due to work stress.

Another important step in addressing work-related stress is to create a team of professionals to develop interventions. The team may need the assistance of outside experts. Colleagues may also be consulted to understand the problem and make recommendations. The team will then design the intervention. They will need to involve different stakeholder groups in the intervention process. The goal is to prevent workplace stress and increase employee productivity so that it doesn't negatively affect the company's bottom line.

In addition to hiring a human resources manager to handle such issues, companies should encourage employee socialization. Increasing communication among colleagues helps prevent work-related stress, as they can share information and offer support if needed.

By developing this kind of stress management policy and seeking advice from health professionals, companies can reduce the burden over time and improve employee morale.

The most effective prevention of workplace stress is a comprehensive program that works on multiple levels. Individual-level interventions are more effective than those that deal with specific causes of workplace stress. Incorporating these strategies into a comprehensive program is the best way to ensure long-term, sustainable results.

There are two primary strategies in preventing workplace stress: **education** and **training**.

Employees can learn from experience and implement it in the workplace. In the latter case, the overall authority and responsibility for the prevention program should remain with the company. Organizations can provide employees with training aimed at preventing workplace stress.

It is important to assess the **level of awareness**, identify the risks, and implement the chosen management intervention. The final step will be to assess the effectiveness of the program.

Some companies may implement a risk assessment process to identify the most effective interventions. A successful prevention program can improve morale and reduce costs. Involving employees in developing a program can also enhance morale and reduce health and safety issues. Getting support is essential. While this might be a daunting task, starting a healthy workplace stress management strategy will benefit the entire company.

Understanding and balancing competing demands are crucial for workplace stress prevention. Identifying and understanding the source of stress and developing clear values is essential to successfully implement effective interventions. It is also important to understand all the possible causes for effective implementation. If the cause isn't clearly defined, a treatment plan can be devised to reduce the effects and the costs.

A good **treatment strategy** is a combination of different approaches. Although research on the prevention of workplace stress has been conducted for several decades, its results are not conclusive. In general, the most effective prevention of workplace stress involves combining structural changes and individual support. However, this approach may be inadequate for some workers, so it is imperative to prioritize the actions of a company in preventing stress related to the employees.

*It is essential to make sure that employees feel confident in their abilities and are happy with their jobs.*

## Managing Work Stress by Organizing Time

Time management is crucial to managing work stress. Having a **list of priorities** that separates "shoulds" from "musts" will make the tasks you're doing more manageable. You can put the "should" at the bottom of your list and delete those you don't have time for. Plan to have regular breaks and avoid running late. Take at least a 20-minute break between each working section and try to schedule lunchtime away from your desk.

When it comes to managing work stress, it's essential to take actions that will improve your mental and physical health. If you're physically and emotionally healthy, you'll be able to cope with stress better, and if you do your part well, you'll feel better and be more productive.

Using **time management** software can also help you manage your stress effectively. By using a program, you'll be able to set priorities that you can use in the future to reduce work-related stress and organize your time. When you schedule your work, you'll have more time to relax and pursue personal interests.

You can schedule your tasks so you can do them in batches and reduce the workload. When you effectively manage your time, you'll find yourself less stressed and more productive. By ensuring you're always on top of your tasks, you'll be better able to focus on your goals and achieve them.

When you organize your time, you'll accomplish more tasks and be more efficient. Organizing will also help you focus on the important things and let go of the insignificant ones. By now, you should know that having too many tasks to do at once will only result in wasting time.

A better time management system will also allow you to take care of your personal life without being distracted by your work. When you're stressed at work, you might not have time for important things in your life, such as exercise or family.

According to the APA, more than half of American adults are suffering from high levels of work-related stress. To combat this, improve your time management. You'll be able to accomplish more without the stress of working longer hours.

Managing work stress is an essential aspect of good health. It's easy to become overwhelmed with work, and the pressure you feel is real and harmful. Managing work stress improves your health and productivity.

The best way to manage your time is to be **efficient**. Improved efficiency leads to more productivity, and your work will be more enjoyable. You'll save time by automating processes and focusing on priorities.

For instance, if you're constantly checking emails, it's time to manage your daily tasks. You can set up a schedule for each of your clients. This way, you will be able to spend more time with friends and family and be more active at work.

Organizing your time is a great way to manage work stress. It will help you stay on track and not lose track of your priorities.

## Tips for Managing Time to Reduce Stress at Work

Have a **balanced work-life**. Burnout is possible when you do too much. You should find a balance between family, work, social activities, solitary pursuits, daily responsibilities, and downtime.

**Get up earlier** in the morning. A mere 10–15 minutes can make a difference between being rushed and having enough time to relax. You can set your watches and clocks fast—a little above normal time —to ensure you don't run late.

Try having your work-hour lunch away from your workstation. This will allow you to relax, recharge, and be more active.

Set healthy boundaries. Too many people feel pressured to be online 24/7. They keep checking their smartphone for updates and messages. It's important to set healthy boundaries when you aren't working or thinking about work.

You should also try not to always take your job home. Also, avoid checking email or answering work calls at night or on weekends.

Do not overcommit. Try to avoid scheduling multiple tasks at once. Make a distinction between "shoulds" and "musts" if you have too many things on your plate.

# Problem-Solving

In the workplace, problem-solving is an essential skill to have. It improves communication and accelerates the process of finding solutions to problems. The more you practice, the more naturally you will find solutions to problems.

Here are some tips to help you become a better problem-solver:

Start with a specific problem and work from there. This technique is not difficult to learn. It is also a good way to improve communication in your workplace. You can practice problem-solving exercises with colleagues or even with yourself. Identifying the problem is the first step in problem-solving. For example, if you are teaching a writing class, you may need to help students improve their skills. To do this, you will go over their writing tests and look for areas in which the students need to improve. You might notice that some of the students struggle with writing paragraphs, while others have trouble structuring sentences. To help them overcome this, you will work with them on constructing paragraphs and sentences.

Learning to **recognize trends** in the environment is another important skill. Using your problem-solving skills to identify the causes and effects of future events allows you to predict and influence the probability of them occurring. With this knowledge, you can even change the impact of the future. Being proactive is a key attribute of a problem-solver. For example, you can change the way you think about problems. This can help you improve your performance and make your team more effective.

# 7

# Stress Management in the Family

There are many ways to manage stress in the family. However, some methods are better suited for some situations than others. For example, a family can work together to determine the causes of stress and find ways to reduce it. Individuals should recognize the effects of stress, such as unhealthy choices and negative reactions. Families should also be encouraged to be physically active, whether through walking, biking, or participating in other outdoor activities. Likewise, children should be encouraged to eat healthy foods and get plenty of exercise. In addition to these methods, psychologists can help families overcome unhealthy patterns and improve their overall health. Some of the strategies include the following:

- Setting daily goals
- Communicating with loved ones
- Building a support system
- Delegating responsibilities
- Avoiding technology

For instance, disconnecting from electronics, such as the TV, cell phones, and computers, can reduce stress on a family. It is important to have a strong support system and set goals for each day. Parents can also help children deal with the effects of stress.

Children's triggers for stress can be very similar to those of adults. Listen to your child and learn about their experiences. If they have trouble coping with stress, try to be supportive and understand their concerns. A calm, caring parent can help children cope with their feelings and problems. It will also allow children to develop better.

A healthy approach to managing stress in the family can help children develop the necessary skills to deal with the situation.

In the first phase, it is crucial to identify the causes of stress in the family. The problem is that unhealthy stress management often leads to negative results for children. It can even lead to the deterioration of the entire family. The only way to prevent a stressed-out family is to learn how to manage stress constructively and healthily.

A healthy dinner with a family activity can help everyone cope with the stress. Eating a healthy dinner and having plenty of exercise will reduce anxiety and stress in children. By implementing some simple strategies, parents can reduce their children's stress levels. By focusing on their children's physical needs, the family will feel less stressed. When parents focus on improving the mental aspects of their family life, they will have more energy and be more likely to enjoy life.

Another great way to help kids cope with stress is to start a family book club. Choosing books together is an excellent way to bond with your spouse and children. The process of reading is also beneficial for children, especially when they are young. This will encourage them to love books and lead to a better understanding of the world around them.

For the most part, reading can help reduce the stress levels of all family members and can make the whole family more relaxed. Stress management in the family can be as simple as making a change in the environment. Children tend to mirror their environment, and a clutter-filled environment can make kids more stressed. By taking the time to clear the home, parents will help their children focus on what they can control instead of what they can't.

When children see that their parents are stressed out, they may make unhealthy choices, such as not eating enough food or being too lazy. Learning how to deal with stress in the family is an important part of a healthy lifestyle. It's important to understand the causes of stress in your family and tailor your message to their level. The best way to teach your children to cope with stress is to make them aware of their strengths and weaknesses and empower them to handle the challenges of everyday life. By providing them information about how to handle their stress, they will be better able to handle the pressures of everyday life.

There are several other ways to relieve stress in the family. By teaching your children positive coping skills, you can help them reduce their stress. For example, they can learn to express their feelings and tell you when they feel stressed.

When children are anxious and feel overwhelmed, they can be too demanding. When a child's stress is caused by a traumatic experience, the parent should make sure that the child feels safe and well understood.

## Stress Treatment Strategies and Techniques

Stress and anxiety reduction are the reason pharmaceutical companies have global marketing capabilities. They do extensive and expensive research and then sell their products through pharmacies after being tested on animals and humans. Prescription medication for anxiety and stress management has a problem. Some people will not be able to reduce their stress/anxiety with the prescribed dosage levels.

Are legally prescribed pills, marijuana, and alcohol the answer? I will say no to alcohol and marijuana (also known as cannabis, weed, grass, joint, Maryjane, and locoweed). In trying to control your stress levels and anxiety, prescription drugs should only be used if your doctor has decided that you are unable to do your daily tasks without them. Your physician will be in touch with you to ensure that prescription drugs are only used within a prescribed timeframe and in the prescribed dosages. Sometimes, the medication may also be used in conjunction with psychotherapy. There are many advertisements on the internet that offer drugs without prescriptions. You're strongly discouraged from taking them as they may be harmful to you.

## Cannabis, Alcohol, and Prescribed Drugs

It is easy to reach for alcohol when under intense anxiety and uncontrollable stress. Alcohol could be in the form of wine, beer, or whiskey. Alcohol is legalized in most Western and Eastern cultures, but not among Muslims. It has a calming effect on the nervous system that lessens tensions and stress; however, it can also become a dangerous substance if consumed too frequently and in large amounts. A Japanese proverb states, "At the start, I take one drink, then the drink takes another drink, and finally, the drink takes me."

---

*"At the start, I take one drink, then the drink takes another drink, and finally the drink takes me."*

---

Sometimes, people also choose to lessen their stress by accepting the rolled marijuana joint or the grass cigarette that their host or friend graciously gives them at a party.

## How Diet Can Help

A healthy and balanced diet is essential to managing the physiological changes triggered by stress. Recognizing and reducing stress is an important part of any stress response. Blood sugar levels have a significant impact on adrenal function; therefore, much of the dietary advice provided below is designed to stabilize sugar levels:

- Select whole food to ensure that you eat at least five portions of non-starchy vegetables per day.
- Get started with a healthy breakfast, and avoid sugary pastries, sugary cereals, and excessive caffeine.
- Prioritize protein. The body's need for protein is higher when it is chronically stressed. The daily protein requirement is 0.7–1.8 grams for every kilogram of body weight. Choose lean meats, poultry, fish, eggs, and legumes in each meal. The release of sugar into your bloodstream is slowed by protein.
- Balance your protein and carbohydrates.
- Don't skip meals. Take healthy snacks whenever you need them. Regular small meals can help you maintain your energy and mood while reducing tiredness and irritability.
- Avoid refined foods like white bread, pasta, chocolate, biscuits, and sweets. Hidden sugars can also be found in bread, cereals, tinned produce, processed or packaged foods, and many other products.
- Replace processed foods with unrefined foods, such as brown bread and rice.
- You should also be aware that excessive alcohol can lead to an imbalance in blood sugar levels.
- Keep a check on the caffeine. While stimulants like tea and coffee can provide an energy boost for a short time, too much could cause a decrease in energy and decrease nutrients over the long term.

- Drink at 1–11.5 liters of filtered drinking water each day. You can also incorporate herbal or fruit teas into your daily water intake.
- Avoid emotional eating. When you're stressed, don't just reach for your food. Stress can divert blood flow when you're trying to digest your food. You might feel gas, bloating, or discomfort.

## Key Nutrients

These nutrients are specifically designed to support the adrenal cells:

- Vitamin C is found in almost all fresh fruits and vegetables. It is found in the adrenal gland and is necessary to produce cortisol.
- Magnesium can be severely depleted during times of stress. Symptoms of deficiency include anxiety, insomnia, fatigue, and predispositions to stress. To ensure adequate magnesium levels, eat plenty of dark-green leafy vegetables and whole grains, as well as nuts, seeds, and legumes.
- B vitamins can support adrenal function, especially $B_5$, which directly supports the adrenal cortex. Whole grains, seeds, and nuts are all good sources.

# 8

# How to Make Self-Care a Priority

Committing to making self-care a priority is not easy. The first steps might feel overwhelming, and you may not be sure where to start. There are many ways to improve your health and well-being. Here are some tips:

- Identify your favorite activities.
- Try to think of things that make you happy, and then choose those activities and schedule them into your daily routine.

This will help you make them a priority. You will have more time to devote to other things, too. First of all, schedule some time for self-care each week. It is essential to set aside a certain amount of time for this activity and make it a habit.

You can also try to schedule it in your calendar. However, if you cannot afford to schedule an hour for yourself every week, you can always opt for a few minutes for yourself during the day. You can treat yourself to a nice hot shower or so.

Self-care is essential for your health and happiness. When you prioritize other things before your own needs, you will feel less happy and more stressed. The best way to start is by scheduling self-care activities throughout the day. Spread them out over a week or a month to maximize your time.

This will make them more enjoyable and easier to adhere to. Regardless of the activity, you must do it regularly. To make self-care a priority, start by setting small goals each day. The goal shouldn't be too difficult, as you can always add more. It will take a while for the habit to take hold. Having a goal to follow every day can help you feel more fulfilled and happier, and if you set a schedule that incorporates self-care, you'll find it easier than ever to stick to it. Self-care is an essential part of your overall well-being. Perhaps create time to spend alone in a natural environment, like a park, to reflect on your life.

While it may seem like a luxury for some, it will help you feel better overall. Oftentimes, a simple activity such as reading a book or listening to music can reduce stress and help you feel good. By making time for yourself, you'll be more effective in coping with stressful situations and managing your day. This will benefit not only you but also everyone around you.

In all you do, remember to drink plenty of water. It is not fun to drink too much water. You should drink at least eight glasses of water each day. By following these guidelines, you'll feel better and be able to keep a healthy balance. You might also want to prioritize self-care by engaging in activities you enjoy.

Most importantly, connect with others. Whether it is with friends or family, the time spent with loved ones can be very uplifting. It can be as simple as inviting a friend over for dinner. You can also host a dinner party with your family and invite your friends over. This will allow you to bond with other people.

By doing things that you enjoy, you are already practicing self-care. Whether it's a relaxing walk or a movie marathon, you'll be more likely to take care of yourself.

## Physical Activities and Stress Relief

Regularly participating in physical activity can help reduce anxiety and lower stress levels. Walking, playing tennis, or taking a meditative walk can also provide a relaxing experience. Other recommended stress-relief activities include meditation, yoga, swimming, or talking to friends. Combining aerobic exercise and relaxing activities can help you find your groove again.

Walking or biking is a great way to clear your mind and reduce stress. If you have time, take a class or join a fitness club. The goal is to build mental and physical fitness.

A healthy mind requires physical activity. The benefits of regular activity are well-known. A well-balanced mind can be the basis for a happier and more successful life. It is important to choose a stress-relief activity that suits your level of physical and emotional well-being. A well-rounded program will provide the most beneficial results.

If you're not very in tune with strength exercises, you can try the **breathing technique.** Breathe deeply and then slowly breathe out. Another way is taking yourself away from the situation. Not thinking about the problem will help you relax, in addition to deep breathing.

You can also **stretch the muscles** in your body. When you do this, you will release tension in the muscle groups of the legs and the thighs. Once you have completed the exercise, the muscles in your body will relax. Repeat this exercise every day for a week or so.

There are many other techniques you can try, but the above-mentioned are a great place to start as you explore more techniques.

I love **meditation**. This method is an effective way to learn to manage stress. It helps you think about and perceive stressful situations in a certain way. By doing this, you can avoid negative emotions and negative thinking patterns, especially if you love spirituality. What do you think about it? In meditating for a few minutes each day, you can start by visualizing a calm, serene place or anything that should meet your fancy. You can then repeat the exercise as many times as you need to. Creating a list of accomplishments in your memory is excellent to do. By tracking your achievements, you will make your soul hardier.

The **progressive muscle relaxation** technique also helps you relax and stay calm. Once you learn and choose a particular technique, you can practice it every day to help you get rid of your stress and stay away from the negative effects of stress. In all these, learn to set realistic goals to manage a stressful situation.

There are numerous ways to manage stress, but no technique is 100 percent effective. By making it a daily routine, you can prevent the onset of stress and prevent it from worsening.

Journaling also helps you understand your feelings and equally gets rid of stress. Writing down your thoughts and feelings is helpful because it allows you to identify the causes of the stressors.

If you're unable to change your circumstances after applying some of these techniques, you can try changing who you are relating to. If you find yourself constantly being irritated by a person, it might be a good idea to cut off your relationship with them. This is a stress management technique that can work for you in many ways. But whatever you do, don't forget to give yourself some time off.

A stress management technique may seem a bit unconventional, but if it's a proven method that helps people cope with daily pressure, then you can consider it.

While traditional methods of psychotherapy are largely okay, alternative methods have been gaining in popularity in recent years. A common management technique that has been widely advised is changing your thoughts and behaviors.

You can combine different techniques until you find the one that works for you. People are different, so it is not a one-size-fits-all approach but a holistic approach to a healthy life.

If someone is causing you too much stress, try to limit your contact with them. Don't spend too much time with the person to avoid triggering a negative impact on your health.

Fortunately (or I guess you already know), there are many apps to help you manage your stress. Some of these apps will allow you to meditate anywhere that suits the quietness that you desire. Some people believe that compiling a list of new things you want to learn can help. Learning new things has a way of motivating people.

Just use whatever is available in solving the perceived problem and the one that helps you accept what you cannot change.

Let me also emphasize that **keeping a journal** that helps you track how you feel at each point in your daily life is a good thing. It's easy to forget how you felt the previous day. Keeping a journal is a great way to track how you feel every day. It will greatly help you identify the things that cause you stress and those that work best for you.

*So you can avoid particular situations from reoccurring in the future.*

These things work in almost all kinds of issues, whether you are an employee in a corporate environment or a freelancer working remotely. There is always a way to manage stress and stay focused.

Remember to always appreciate yourself and the work you do. You can give your soul more purpose and increase your drive to succeed.

Always learn to avoid distractions so you can finish a particular thing and still have time for other important things.

## Meditation

Meditation is a practice that has been used for thousands of years. Meditation was originally intended to deepen our understanding of the sacred, mystical, and spiritual forces of life. Meditation is now used to relax and reduce stress. It can be considered a form of mind-body medicine. It can help you relax and calm your mind. It helps you focus your attention on the present moment and removes any clutter or distracting thoughts from your mind. This leads to better physical and emotional well-being.

Meditation has many benefits. It can help you feel calm, peaceful, and balanced. It will benefit your mental well-being and your overall health. These benefits do not end after your meditation session is over.

Meditation can improve your emotional well-being, and meditation can help you get rid of the information overload that builds up each day and contributes to stress.

Meditation can help with stress and anxiety. Although there is increasing evidence supporting meditation's health benefits, others believe it is impossible to prove its benefits.

Research suggests meditation can help with conditions such as allergies, anxiety disorders, asthma, cancer, depression, fatigue, heart disease, high blood pressure, pain, sleep problems, and substance abuse. Meditation should not be used in place of traditional medical treatment. It can be an addition to other treatments, though.

## Stress, Meditation, and PTSD

Regular meditation has helped many in decreasing the impact of chronic health problems like anxiety, depression, pain, nausea/vomiting due to cancer treatment, or post-traumatic syndrome disorder (PTSD). A recent survey showed that 84 percent improved their concentration after doing mindfulness exercises for just 30 minutes per day over two weeks! In addition, researchers have found that people who practice mindfulness regularly have **improved memory** function.

**Stress is mostly an internal response to a perceived threat or need**. Thus, it is usually caused by the thoughts that respond to a threat. These thoughts cause physical, mental, and emotional upset. The immediate result is a rapid heartbeat, shallow breathing, and surging adrenalin.

To effectively carry out meditation, you will need a quiet place. This should not be hard. All you need is a comfortable chair or a reclining seat. If you think lying down on a bed or sofa is easier, you can do so as long as it relaxes your body.

The best way to start is by focusing on the present moment and paying attention to the physical sensations. Once you've mastered this technique, you can start to practice it regularly. If you've never meditated before, you must try doing something in that regard and feel the amazing results. With time, you will make the practice a habit. You may want to start meditating every day for, say, at least five minutes.

So many types of meditation are available, so you can find one that is suitable for your needs. A lot of videos are available online in this regard.

You may have a little difficulty mastering any kind of meditation that you have chosen, but it will become easier. While the practice may be a little intimidating for many people, they're often surprised at how quickly they're able to manage the stress that made them start the process. Good meditation practice will teach you to focus and let go of negative thoughts and feelings. The more you practice, the more you'll notice that your stress level is dropping.

Those who meditate before sleeping at night have reported better overnight sleep, better health, and a happier and more contented life. It is useful in reducing **blood lactate levels** and improving the cardiovascular system. Whether you choose to meditate for health or stress management, the resultant effect is always good.

It is also found to help in improving one's self-esteem. The most important thing to remember is that the more you practice it, the more it will stick with you. The practice of meditation can help you achieve a sense of inner peace, and just about anyone can learn to do it.

## Different Types of Meditation

**Guided imagery** (also known as visualization) is a method of meditation that allows you to create mental images of situations or places you find relaxing. It is important to make use of all your senses during this process. You may be guided by a teacher or so.

**Mantra meditation** is a type of meditation that involves silent repetition of a calming thought, word, or phrase to take your mind away from distracting thoughts. Mindfulness meditation is about being mindful of and accepting the present moment. You also broaden your consciousness. It is possible to observe thoughts and emotions but not judge them.

**Qi gong** is another method of meditation that combines relaxation, meditation, movement, and breathing exercises to help restore and maintain equilibrium. Traditional Chinese medicine includes *qi gong* (*CHEE-gung*). *Tai chi* (pronounced *TIE-chee*) is a gentle Chinese martial art that involves slow, graceful movements and slow, controlled postures.

**Transcendental meditation** works by narrowing your awareness and removing all thoughts from your head, and you use a mantra to do this. It can be a word, sound, or phrase repeated silently. To achieve perfect stillness and consciousness, you must focus solely on your mantra.

**Yoga** is another method of meditation. You'll find that you can focus more on the present moment and less on your busy days as you do poses that require balance.

## Meditation Elements

Different meditation styles may have different features that can help you meditate. These features may differ depending on who is giving the class or who you are following. Below are the most important features of meditation:

**Focused attention** is a practice that requires you to do as it says—focus your attention. Your mind will be free from all distractions that cause stress and worry. Focusing your attention can be done by focusing on a specific object, an idea, a mantra, or your breathing.

**Relaxed breathing** is a technique that uses deep, slow breathing to expand your lungs. This technique will slow down your breathing, increase oxygen intake, and reduce muscle use in the neck, shoulder, and upper chest while allowing you to breathe more efficiently.

**A quiet setting** can be more enjoyable for beginners if there are no distractions, such as televisions, radios, or cell phones. You may find it easier to meditate anywhere as you become more proficient, particularly in stressful situations, like being in traffic or long lines at the grocery store.

Whether you are sitting, standing, or walking, a **comfortable position** is a must while doing meditation. To get the best out of meditation, you should be comfortable. Don't let stress arise from meditating. You can go to special meditation classes or take part in group classes with trained instructors. You can also practice meditation on your own. Depending on your situation and lifestyle, meditation can be as informal or formal as you wish, and it can be perfectly integrated into your daily life.

---

*The best forms of self-meditation are those that may not require an instructor, and you can do it whenever you want.*

---

**Deep breathing** is best for beginners as breathing is a natural function. Concentrate all your attention on your breathing, and inhale and exhale through the nostrils. Deepen your breathing slowly and deeply. If your attention wanders, return to your breathing.

**Take a look at your body**, as this allows you to focus your attention on its different parts. Be aware of the different sensations your body is experiencing, such as pain, tension, warmth, or relaxation. Combining body scanning and breathing exercises helps you imagine yourself bringing relaxation into different parts of the body.

**Repeat a mantra**. No matter what religion you're practicing, there's always a mantra available that you can adopt. In Christianity, an example of a religious mantra is the "Jesus Prayer." There are also many mantras in Judaism, Hinduism, Buddhism, and other Eastern religions.

**Take a walk and meditate.** Combining walking and meditation can be a healthy and efficient way to relax. This technique can be used whether you are in a peaceful forest, on a sidewalk, or at the mall. This technique allows you to slow down your pace so you can concentrate on the movements of your feet and legs. You will be focusing on the journey and not the destination.

**Prayer** is the most well-known and widely used form of meditation. Most faith and traditions have both spoken and written prayers. Prayers can be recited in your own words, or you can read prayers from others. Ask your priest, pastor, or spiritual leader for information about resources.

**Reflect and read.** Many people find that reading sacred texts or poems can help them relax and reflect. Listening to sacred music, inspiring words, or relaxing music is another option. You may also write down your thoughts in a journal or share them with a friend afterward.

**Concentrate on your gratitude and love.** When you focus your attention on a sacred being or object, it weaves feelings of love into your thoughts. You can also close your eyes and focus on the object or use your imagination to look at images of it. Your meditation skills are important. Don't be afraid to practice meditation. Meditation must be done with constant practice for full effectiveness. It is normal for your mind and body to wander while you meditate, regardless of how many years you have been doing it. When you meditate to calm your mind and your attention wanders, you can slowly return to the object or sensation you are focusing on.

You'll discover what meditation works best for you when you do the one you like doing. You can adapt meditation to suit your current needs. There is not a right or wrong way to meditate.

# Abdominal Breathing

Observe your breathing. Place one hand on your chest and the other on your abdomen. Which is moving faster, your abdomen or chest? **Abdominal breathing** is where your abdomen moves more than your chest. Deep abdominal breathing is a natural method of breathing. This can be observed by lying down on your back and focusing on your breathing. You'll probably notice that your abdomen moves more than your chest. You might also notice a relaxation in your abdomen as you continue to breathe.

## How We Breathe

Your torso is divided into two areas: the upper (chest) area (the area that contains your heart and lungs) and the lower (abdomen) area. The diaphragm is the primary muscle that allows you to breathe. It stretches across your midsection and separates the abdomen from the chest. When we breathe in, the diaphragm contracts and the ribs expand. This causes the chest to grow and the lungs to fill with air. The diaphragm relaxes downward, and the ribs pull in. This reduces the chest size and pushes the air out of our lungs.

## Stress and Breathing

Our bodies can respond to stress by having rapid, shallow breathing. People may experience shallow breathing—holding their breath when under stress. This could be due to habitual tension or anxiety. This can be correctly observed by tightening your abdominal muscles and breathing deeply. Holding your stomach in place will prevent the diaphragm's full downward contraction.

Neck and shoulder tension can be caused by breathing only with your chest. Tight clothing around the waist prevents the stomach from expanding during inhalation, and thinking you have to keep your stomach in contributes to shallow breathing. Focusing on your breathing can help you relax during stressful times.

You can correct this by always wearing comfortable clothing and maintaining a good posture that allows you to breathe in your abdomen. It may feel awkward to begin abdominal breathing while lying down. It will become better and easier to practice abdominal breathing as you continue practicing. You can also use abdominal breathing to relax and manage stress.

**9**

# Stress-Free Actions

The benefits of stress-free actions are numerous. Getting outside to enjoy the fresh air and vitamin D is very good. You need to love natural beauty as it has a way of improving mental health. If you're worried about your daily routine, try these stress-relieving activities to make the day more bearable.

If you can't find anything to do at some point, start writing out ideas. Writing your thoughts can help you gain insight and become more creative. You can try to give yourself a stress-free task to complete, and it can be anything from completing a puzzle to organizing shoes. Whatever you choose to do, don't forget to enjoy it.

You can do things for yourself or someone else. Regardless of your personal preferences, there are many ways to get your mind off your stressful job. It's important to listen to your body to prevent burnout.

## The Benefits of Creating a Stress Journal

In addition to keeping a diary, creating a stress journal can help you identify your stress patterns. Writing about your experiences can help you become aware of how you react to stressors and develop coping strategies. If you're experiencing excessive stress, you may need to make some changes in your habits and mindset.

Creating a daily stress journal can help you become more resilient to stressors, and it can help you feel better when you're feeling stressed out. Keeping a stress journal can help you recognize the sources of your stress.

Having an ongoing record of your feelings and responses to stressors can help you develop new ways to deal with stressful situations. The benefits of maintaining a journal are numerous.

Paying attention to your responses will ultimately improve your health and work performance. Once you've found your stress triggers, you can identify the best way to deal with them.

Creating a stress journal can help you identify the things that make you feel stressed so that you can deal with them. The more you write, the more likely you are able to notice them and deal with them.

It will also help you recognize patterns and improve your sleeping habits, improving overall mental health. It helps you develop coping mechanisms.

## Managing Your Thoughts to Manage Stress

Managing your thoughts is an important aspect of effective stress management. The first step is to become aware of your thoughts and their patterns. Try to accept them without judgment. By identifying what makes you think in a certain way, you can take steps to change your negative thoughts. You can even change how you think about stressful situations if you are aware of the cause.

The source of the problem is usually in your mind. Managing your thoughts can help you overcome stress caused by past or future events. When negative thoughts keep replaying over and over in your head in an endless loop, they can cause you to worry and become stressed.

Repeated thoughts are counterproductive to coping with stress. You should try to replace your negative thinking with positive thoughts. Practicing gratitude can help you deal with negative thoughts. Once you can control your thoughts, you will feel happier and more relaxed.

Another way to manage your thoughts is to keep a journal, as stated earlier. Writing down your thoughts about stress triggers will help you identify the most common causes of your stress. It will also be easier to pinpoint the specific patterns that cause you the most stress. This way, you can avoid triggering them with more positive messages and habits.

Managing your thoughts to manage stress starts with identifying the sources of your stress. You can identify the major stressors easily, but chronic stressors are more difficult to identify.

Procrastination is the source of chronic stress. Taking steps to stop procrastination will help you control your stress. Using gratitude to reduce your overall stress will increase your sense of well-being too. When it comes to reducing stress, you should learn how to control your thoughts.

When you have an uncontrollable situation, it may become more difficult to deal with, which will lead you to make poor choices. So, instead of focusing on the source of your stress, focus on what you can control.

You will notice that creeps in when you start thinking about past or future events. These thoughts can create an endless cycle of worries, so it's important to become aware of these thoughts and learn how to manage them to reduce the effects of stress.

You'll find that you can manage your stress effectively by controlling what goes through your mind at any moment.

Managing your thoughts to manage stress is not an easy task. It requires practice, discipline, and commitment; however, if you do it diligently, you will gradually decrease unnecessary thoughts and emotions in the best way possible.

Avoid people with negative attitudes as they will make you more stressed and doubt your ability to manage issues. When these thoughts occur, focus on what you can control instead; it will help you to stay positive and calm at all times.

## Developing Stress-Free Thinking

A major reason why we're stressed is that we're too busy worrying about the next big thing. It is a fact that we spend more time working than sleeping. We work 2,000 to 4,000 hours a year. This amount of time is a considerable investment, and it is often counterproductive not to improve your mental health by focusing on other things.

By developing stress-free thinking, you can reduce your daily stress levels and create a happier and more peaceful existence.

One of the easiest ways to get rid of stress is to practice kindness. By performing one act of kindness every day, you'll be reducing your stress levels. This kind of action doesn't have to be expensive or complicated. It can be as simple as wishing someone a happy birthday. It is a great way to reduce the impact of negative thinking on your health.

The most effective way to do this is by establishing a daily habit of being kind. Maintaining a daily habit of doing something kind to someone else or a random stranger can significantly reduce your stress levels.

It's a good idea to do a kind act, no matter what. You may have heard of people who made a birthday card for someone who doesn't deserve it or give them a present for their birthday. This helps the person giving the card or gift. Another idea is that if you are frustrated about someone's behavior, you can leave the room to calm down and return to do something kind to them. It's a great way to lift your spirits.

Many people can't imagine that giving someone a nice gift might just do the magic. When you have a sense of gratitude, you can make people feel better, and you, too, will feel happier and more fulfilled.

Creative activities are regarded as positive actions that can make anyone happy. You can try exploring some of them to your advantage. Instead of yelling and shouting at others, try to focus on a kind act that can make people feel good. You don't have to be rich or famous to create that kind of atmosphere contrary to what you may be thinking.

Just try to find a way to make someone smile, no matter how small. It won't take much, but it can make a big difference. It will boost your confidence and make you feel more positive. Using kindness to reduce stress is something almost everyone should adopt because it is a healthy habit. It is important to remember that you can choose to focus on the positives in any situation. By focusing on the positive, you will remove the negative energy from your mind and create a stress-free environment.

## Managing Stress With Positive Thinking

Positive thinking will make you see more opportunities in the future, and you will have the mindset to be successful. You will also feel less stressed and more optimistic about life. If you think you're not feeling optimistic, you can start practicing some of the techniques mentioned above. You can practice visualization, which is a powerful technique for overcoming stress. Try visualizing a better future. You will feel better in general. By visualizing success, you will feel more confident and happier. Positive people are more confident and take risks because they see more possibilities. They are open to new opportunities and see many possible solutions to problems.

Thinking positively is a skill you must adopt if you want to be more successful and happier. Besides the aforementioned benefits, positive thinking also helps improve health by reducing the negative effects of stress. It will also improve your personality. Regardless of your personality type, you can develop your skills to think positively in all situations.

Many studies have also suggested that thinking positively can increase your lifespan and satisfaction. You may even be surprised at how much you can achieve when you focus on the positive side of life. Positive thinking pictures goals and aspirations. It adopts most of the techniques mentioned in the basic meditation style. This type of mentality will make you more optimistic and confident. You'll be able to handle negative situations and stress more positively.

But it isn't easy to develop the positive traits required for positive thinking. You can try to develop these skills by consciously putting them into practice. If you are struggling with your negative thoughts, try harder to replace them with positive thoughts. You can't keep thinking negatively without noticing the effect on your body. The same is the case with positive thinking. Having a positive mindset helps you feel happier.

Fortunately, thinking positively is a skill you can practice anywhere— at home, at work, while walking, and even during playtime.

No wonder it is said that once you can change your thinking, you can change your world. It's important to understand that your personality may be the source of your stress because the right mindset will improve your mood and reduce stress.

Positive thinking is a process of reinforcing standards, being mindful of what you are doing and thinking, and pondering problems. When you are aware of your thoughts and actions, you can reshape situations and make them more positive. It helps you focus on the present while ensuring mindfulness of the future. Positive thinking can help you develop new skills to overcome challenges in your life. It is a proven method for boosting self-esteem too.

It is also good to understand the law of attraction. According to this theory, if you believe in something, it will happen. In other words, if you think it will happen, it will. However, it may not be needed in all situations, and its outcome isn't based on any **scientific evidence**. Some experts in psychology consider the law of attraction **pseudoscience**.

Just as when you feel nervous, your body releases adrenaline, which pumps through your system, helping you communicate with greater enthusiasm and intensity. It's the same way that positive thinking can help change your mindset and help you achieve your goals.

Studies have shown that people who practice positive thinking are more likely to develop new skills and improve existing ones. This is why positive thinking is such a powerful tool to improve one's life. When done correctly, it can create a better world and help you live a more fulfilled life. If you're looking for a job or a promotion, it's time to start this way of thinking. Dependable research has also shown that positive thinking can make you more productive and satisfied.

It is easier to get the best out of life when you're confident and happy. It will also help you improve your relationships with others.

It can make you more attractive to others because of that positive disposition. Learn also to support positive action and initiative because thinking is a mere wish, but actions will bring that positive thinking to reality.

There's a subtle way you can condition your mind for good. Things like reading famous psychological books on related topics will help you perfect this lifestyle. A lot of books have been written by leading psychologists on this, and a little research is all you need to do.

These books will provide additional details and perspectives that articles and short reads may not be able to do.

## Managing Stress With Physical Activity

Being active physically has a way of helping you overcome stress. There are many health benefits to physical activity. It's good for the body, and it helps manage stress. Whether you're playing a game of tennis or taking a meditative meander, exercise can help you feel better and get more sleep.

Regardless of your physical fitness level, there's always an activity for you. It doesn't have to be a competitive sport. Just a short walk may be all you need to positively affect your mood.

Research also suggests that almost all types of exercise can help you cope with stress. Walking, jogging, and swimming are just a few to mention.

Physical activities improve mood and can improve your self-esteem. Riebe et al. (2015) found that the best exercises to reduce stress are those that improve muscle strength and endurance, but simple activities can also have a nice impact.

According to a study in the *Journal of American Colleges of Sport and Exercise*, regular physical exercise can significantly improve stress and well-being. It has also been established that regular physical activity reduces mild to moderate levels of anxiety and depression and can improve sleep.

It typically increases the level of endorphins—chemicals produced by the brain that make people feel good. In their suggestion, the Centers for Disease Control and Prevention advised that adults should engage in at least 30 minutes of aerobic exercise a day at least three times per week.

The most recommended exercise duration is 150 minutes of moderate to vigorous exercise. Shorter sessions of physical activity, such as jogging, walking, and cycling, are recommended.

Whichever type you decide to choose, just know that the aim should be to help you achieve a set target. Adults who regularly exercise are less likely to skip their weekly workouts than those who don't.

Despite the many benefits of physical activity, it's important to find a program that suits you and your lifestyle. By choosing the right exercises, you can avoid stress and improve your mood. Remember, exercising is a healthy habit for all ages.

---

*While you may not be able to exercise every day, a small amount of activity can be beneficial.*

---

Researchers also say that adults who engage in physical activity at least three times per week are more likely to sleep better and experience better mental health. It will also reduce the likelihood of depression and anxiety. There is indeed no better way to manage stress than physical activity. It's also a proven way to keep a body strong, resilient, and happy.

# 10

# Stress Management and Dietary Tips

Stress management requires a healthy diet. A well-balanced meal can reduce the impact of stressful situations on your body. A **balanced meal** is rich in protein, vitamins, and minerals. Lean proteins are good for the adrenal glands. They also help to relax the muscles and keep you alert.

You are required to eat plenty of fruits and vegetables, whole grains, and legumes. Eat foods rich in fiber and foods that are natural antioxidants, like berries, green vegetables, and beans. To state the obvious, eating plenty of fresh fruits and vegetables is one of the best ways to keep your body healthy, and it is particularly important for people with chronic stress.

You have already been told that constant stress impairs the body's immune system and depletes its defenses. This leaves stressed people more susceptible to disease and infection. Getting sick can put even more strain on the body, so eating fruit and vegetables is a great way to boost your health because of its rich dose of vitamins and minerals.

When stress damages the immune system and lowers your body defenses, you will be more vulnerable to infection and disease. As a strategic dietary plan, you must focus on food items that are high in vitamins B and C. In addition to getting enough vitamin C, magnesium, zinc, iron, and fiber should be a priority. Experts say that the body goes into recovery mode during stress, which means it will decrease its metabolism process and increase your appetite. This is not good for the body. Be mindful of what you eat when stressed to avoid eating more calories than you need.

# How to Handle Stress With Sleep

You must, at this point, realize the importance of having enough sleep. Sleep is a natural stress-relieving therapy. Not getting enough sleep is a recipe for stress. If you want to avoid the consequences of not getting enough sleep, you must plan your activities accordingly.

The present pandemic continues to send people into a panic mood, and more people are now working from home. Unfortunately, working from home has a way of making you work long hours, compromising your sleep hours. You need to ensure that you get the proper amount of rest you need.

At this point in your life, you don't need anybody to remind you of the importance of sleep. If you go through 24 hours without sleep, your body will remind you that you're doing something wrong to it.

Stress, often, can make you not want to sleep, but if you can find a way to put yourself to sleep, you may have defeated stress. This is because by the time you wake up from sleep, you will be energized and a little better than before you went to sleep.

Many people who find it difficult to fall asleep do so because they may be worrying too much about work or other personal problems. Even those who manage to get a good night's sleep are entirely free unless they make it a habit to go to bed at the right time. Getting enough sleep has a way of dealing with chronic stress because it is a natural remedy that can help you achieve healthy living. A healthy sleep schedule is important for your health.

If you have difficulty falling asleep, you can try a guided meditation where you will visualize all the tension leaving your body. It will help you to relax.

A night of deep, relaxing sleep will keep you feeling refreshed and rejuvenated. As a good practice, try resting for a while before going to bed. While resting, take your mind away from all your worries so you can concentrate on going to sleep.

You can also learn how to handle your body's arousal. **Arousal** is a natural process that wakes you up when you're afraid of something. It prepares us for fight or flight. While arousal is good for animals, it's not so good for humans as it causes unnecessary stress, so it's best to learn how to handle it.

# Conclusion

Stress can cause more than just temporary pressure. Although stress cannot be avoided, it can be managed, and skills can be developed to deal with stressful situations. You'll be better equipped to help your friends, classmates, and colleagues by learning how to manage stress and recognizing the signs of suicide.

Your stress levels will be out of your control if you don't take measures to control them. Certain coping strategies are ineffective in reducing stress; they can also be more harmful in the long term: Avoid drinking excessively (alcohol), using illegal drugs and pills, sitting in front of a computer or TV for hours, and neglecting friends and family. Choose healthier ways of managing stress. There are many methods to manage stress, and when deciding on a solution, you can either change the situation or create your responses. These four steps are useful:

- Prevent
- Modify
- Adapt
- Accept

There is no single solution to stress because everyone reacts differently to it. In every situation, one method may not be the best. It is important to try different methods and techniques to determine which one makes you feel calm and in control. Avoid unnecessary stress.

Avoiding stressful situations is one way to reduce stress. There are many stressors that you can manage. Learn to say no. Know your limitations. It doesn't matter if it is about personal or professional life. It is the best way to avoid stress. You should avoid people who stress you out. If you can't, try to limit your time with them or end the relationship.

You can control the environment around you. If the evening news makes you anxious, turn off the TV. You can choose a different route if the traffic is causing you stress. You don't have to go to the supermarket every day if you find it difficult. Instead, shop online for groceries. If you and someone else have different beliefs about religion, politics, or other hot topics, avoid discussing them. You should not argue about a topic with others. If it stresses you out every time, then it's time to stop.

Write down all your tasks. Review your daily plans, responsibilities, and tasks. You may have lots of tasks to complete. If this is the case, you can prioritize the most important or remove them from the list. If you cannot change a situation, it is possible to be mindful of how you respond to it. Find out what you can do in the future to ensure that the stressful conditions don't reappear. This often requires a shift in how you communicate with others.

---

*Don't fight with your feelings. Express your feelings if you are upset by someone so you will not make the situation worse.*

---

Accept compromises. You can influence someone's behavior by being open to compromise. You will have a lot of fun together if you are flexible. Be more confident. Don't let your life slip away. You can cope with problems and do your best to eliminate them or prevent them from happening again. Stress can be caused by poor time management. It's impossible to be calm and focused when you're late or running behind schedule on an appointment or a submission. Planning can reduce stress and ensure you have enough time.

If you are unable to change the stressor, adapt! You can adapt to stressful situations and take control of your life by changing your outlook and expectations. You can change the way you view problems. Look at problems with a positive lens.

Consider the time you are stuck in traffic as an opportunity to take a break and listen to your favorite radio station or just enjoy the solitude. Your standards are yours. Perfectionism can cause stress. You don't have to be perfect to be successful. You can set reasonable standards for yourself and others and learn that "relatively good" can be good. Change your outlook. Your mental and physical health can be affected by how you think about it. Your body reacts to negative thoughts by assuming it is in the same situation. You will feel happier if you are positive about yourself.

Accepting the fact that some stress sources are inevitable is important. It is impossible to prevent the death or serious illness of a friend, as well as a national recession. Accepting uncontrollable events is the best way to manage stress. Accepting the uncontrollable may seem difficult, but it will become easier over time. You can't control the uncontrollable, so why stress about them?

There are many things in life that we cannot control, including the behavior of other people. Instead of focusing on them, think about the things you can control—for example, how to solve problems. Learn from your mistakes if your choices cause stress. Talk to someone and share your feelings. Although it doesn't change the situation, this simple action can be extremely beneficial to your mental health.

Talking is not an indication of weakness. Many friends will be glad that you trusted them, which will lift your spirits. Learn forgiveness. Accept that the world is imperfect and that people might be wrong. Be calm and not controlled by your anger.

You can let go of negative emotions and move forward. You can take time to have fun and relax with a positive outlook. This will help you to nurture yourself and decrease stress. You will be able to cope better with stressors in life if you make time for recreation and relaxation. You can relax by walking, talking to your pet, and exercising every day. Do not let the hustle and bustle of daily life overwhelm you. Rest! It is a necessity to nourish your body and soul. Relaxation should be a part of your daily routine. Do not let other things interfere with your me time. This is the best time to let go of all your daily responsibilities and recharge your batteries.

Keep in touch. Your life will be better if you spend time with positive people. It is important to have people who will support you. This will help you avoid the negative effects of stress. Find activities that bring you joy every day. Allow yourself to enjoy your leisure time, even if it's a fantasy. Keep your sense of humor. You can improve your resilience to stress by living a healthy lifestyle.

Regular exercise is key to reducing stress and preventing it from happening. Work out at least 30 minutes a day, three times per week. Aerobic exercise is a great way to relieve stress.

Eat a healthy diet. A healthy body will be better equipped to handle stress. Pay attention to what foods you eat. Start the day with breakfast and continue eating healthy meals throughout the day to boost energy and mental clarity.

Limit your sugar and caffeine intake. While high levels of sugar and caffeine may initially make someone happy, they eventually overwhelm them. You will feel more relaxed and have a better sleep at night if you reduce the intake of sugary drinks, coffee, and synthetic beverages.

Avoid smoking, alcohol, and drug abuse. Self-treatment with alcohol and drugs can be a temporary escape from stress, but it is not a permanent solution. Don't be afraid to confront the problem. Clear your mind and face your problems. Get enough sleep. Your mind is powered by sleep. Your mind is just like your body. It needs fuel and nutrition.